Sister Circle:
The Power Of Sisterhood

A Guide To Becoming The Woman God Designed You To Be.

By Cheryle T. Ricks

PRESS

Copyright © 2013 by Cheryle T. Ricks

Sister Circle: The Power Of Sisterhood
A Guide To Becoming The Woman God Designed You To Be.
by Cheryle T. Ricks

Printed in the United States of America

ISBN 9781628397895

All rights reserved solely by the author. The author guarantees all contents are original and do not infringe upon the legal rights of any other person or work. No part of this book may be reproduced in any form without the permission of the author. The views expressed in this book are not necessarily those of the publisher.

Unless otherwise indicated, Bible quotations are taken from the King James Version, *Public Domain*.

www.xulonpress.com

Cheryle T. Ricks' Story

※

All of my life I have been searching for my identity. I had no self-esteem and no sense of self-worth. Therefore, I looked for my identity in my relationship with men by using my body to give sexual pleasure. During those years, I never knew that I had any other value but my sexuality. That road led me to having three children before graduating from high school and my fourth child before my 20th birthday. I had my first baby at 14 years old and a set of twins before my 18th birthday. Still not learning who I was, I became pregnant again within six weeks of having my twins. I was so disappointed in myself. However, my OBGYN doctor told me that I could not safely carry that baby because I had such a dangerous delivery with my twins. So, at the age of 17 I had an abortion. Still looking for validation, I married the father of my twins because I was convinced that he was a good father to all of my kids including my first son who was not his biological child and he was the first man that I had ever "loved." My mother knew my potential and begged me not to marry him. However, in *my mind, marriage would make me somebody. It didn't matter that he was already physically and emotionally abusing me. Because I had no sense of value, I never took heed to the wisdom of my mother and older sisters. Therefore, I continued to travel that same dead end road and it lead me to five more years of hell.*

Like so many other abused women who couldn't see any light of hope, I cried out to God to help me and He did before I killed my husband and myself, as I had dreamt of doing many times before. However, I had to make a hard choice between escaping the abuse and staying with my children. You see; my husband was a good father and provider, but he was a bad husband. Therefore, I left my children with my husband and ran for my life. However the pain of leaving my kids behind soon landed me in a mental institution for depression. I was a mother with no one to mother. It was my mental health episode that united me with my children and softened my husband's heart. It was then that God took me through the healing process and restored me to the woman He had created me to be.

Even after our divorce, I was able to forgive my husband. We put the past behind us and rebuilt our relationship to co-parent our children. Prior to my husband's death we were the best of friends. My children are now grown and very self-sufficient. Each of them is a blessing to my life!

Because of what I have gone through, I now realize my self-worth and how valuable I am. The things that Satan meant to destroy me with were the very things that have made me who I am. Today, I am an ordained evangelist who shares the hope of Jesus with other women who are also victims of abuse or who just don't know their self-worth. God is allowing me to use this book to help other women realize that with a relationship with God they can transform their lives and become an instrument of hope to others.

Dedication and Acknowledgments

�֍

I dedicate this book to my Lord and Savior; Jesus Christ, who gave me a plan and a hope that could only be found in His love for me.

To my Lord and Savior Jesus Christ, who gave me a burning desire to share His love with others through this book; may each word minister God's love to every woman who reads it.

To sisters: Lorraine Lifsey, Marguerite Hudson, Lynda Thomason, Frances Mealy, my only brother: Joseph James Mealy, Jr. and my brother-in-law: Herbert Hudson. Thank you all for being there during the darkest parts of my life. Your love, support and care, gave me hope when I did not have hope for myself.

To my mother: *Marguerite Edna Spicer Mealy who had the faith to believe that I would one day become the woman I am today. Momma, I still feel your presence with me everyday.*

To my father: *Joseph James Mealy, Sr. who taught me to make do with what I had and make it into what I needed it to be.*

To my daughters: *Chevelle Ricks and Sherelle Ricks, thank you for learning those life lessons sooner than I did and for being further along than I was at your age. May God fulfill His purpose in you!*

To my sons: *Ronald Cowan, Jr. and Larry T. Ricks, Jr. thank you for being the rocks that keeps our family standing strong! You are the pride of our family. May God continue the work He has started in both of you!*

To my grandsons: *Kasshan L. Cowan, Diontay Braheem Ricks, Derek Defortaine Goldsmith, III, Larry T. Ricks, III, and Malik Jauan Hargis. Thank you for the blessings you bring to our family. Each of you is so special and your lives will give our family what we need to stand for future generations!*

To my only grand-daughter: *Aniya Satea Whitfield, may the women you encounter throughout your life provide you with the love and support you need to make you a woman who will help change the world.*

To my dear friends: Candiesas Harris, Cathy Dixon-Kheir, Cheryl Ann Scott, Louise F. Jones, Marie Minor, Michele Savage and Michele Turner and Sibil Thomas, thank you for always being a true friend and blessing to my life. I thank God for you all!

To my dearest friend: Francis Charles Snyder, thank you for helping me see my true beauty and for all of your support and confidence in me. I thank God for all you bring to my life!

To Literary Team: Rudy Coleman, Cathy Dixon-Kheir, Cheryl Ann Scott, Bishop Matthew E. Bradby, II, Erika Bennett, Francis C. Snyder, Kendall Foster, Kimberly Shipley, Maxine Cunningham, Monique Stubbs-Hall, and P. Irene Jones. Thank you for helping me take the steps to make this book a reality. Your support and guidance made this book possible.

To My Mentors and Coaches
Bishop Matthew E. Bradby II, Rudy Coleman, Marcus Logan, Lynae Turner, Pastor Joyce Meyer, Bishop Noel Jones, Bishop T. D. Jakes and Pastor Creflo Dollar. Thank you so much for helping to bring out the best in me and for all of the encouragement you gave me every step of the way!

To great niece: Jaelyn Zoie' Lee. Thank you for sharing your love with me when I needed it the most!

To Dr. Harini Balu: *Thank you for being a constant blessing in my life. I could not have come this far without your support and guidance.*

To My Sister Circle: *Adelaide Addie Anderson, Alma Maybane, Amina T. Johnson, Andrea Young, Angela Edges, Angela Morris, Anissa Goldring, Anita Goldring, Audrey Huka, Augusta Siribuo, Beverley Gilchrist, Bonnie Coleman, Brandi Stocksdale, Brenda Arthur, Brenda Baskins, Candice Bradby, Carolyn Baker, Carolyn Ward, Cathy Fox, Cecelia Amos-Blanks, Cecelia Campbell, Chante Tindal, Chinyere Okiyi, Cornelia Kruse', Cynthia Perkins, Cynthia Tatum-Jordan, Dalphne Chatman-Hanks, Debra McKenna, Delores Johnson, Diana Donoho, Donna Price, Ellistine Green, Emily Harris, Erika Bennett, Erin Lemon, Eunice Stokes, Felicia Atugbokoh-Biokoro, Frances Radford, Gladys Ellerby, Glynis Monk, Gwendolyn Mayo, Ina Dorsey, Ivel Arbuhah, Jacqueline Augustine, Jacqueline Burkett, Janice Lee, Jennifer Francis, Jillian Clarke, Joi Dyson, Joy Ukpong, Juanita Dixon-Jeffers, Juliana Jack, Kamilah Similey, Kathryn Petrarca, Kay Rice, Kelly Gucwa, Kelly Johnson, Kentilia Patterson, Kia Eason, Kimyetta Holder, Leah Grady, Lillian Williams, Lynda Williams, Madeline Garrett, Manzar Rassouli, Marcella Howard, Marie Foreman, Mary Ann Ervin, Mary Clark, Mary Lee, Mary Plunkett, Mia Dudley, Michelle Moore, Melissa Powell, Melissa Taylor, Michelle Godfrey, Monica Hardy, Monique Ellis, Mother Rosa Faircloth, Naasira Muhammad, Nelwyn Henry , Pamela Bishop, Pamela Biagas, Patricia Lesley, Patricia Sparrow, Pauline Kwenah, Pearl Ewuzie, Pecolia Silver, Quiana*

Preston, Robin Cash, Ravital Shalev, Rebecca Cole, ReVonda Washington, Rubie Meekins, Sarita Herrera, Shameka Powell, Sharon Blakely, Sharon Dennis, Sharon Ozel, Shelane Bell, Shelena Wright-Sanderson, Shelia Harris, Sherri Ford, Sylvia Barrett, Syreeta Eldridge, Tamara Moore, Tamara Sutton, Tameka Fuller, Tami Morningstar, Tanya Keene, Tenia Edwards-Allen, Theresa Ejionye, Theresa Lee, Tia Blue, Tracie Cobb, Valerie Robinson, Vanessa Smith, Veronica Ackie, Veronica Stanton, Wanda Allen, Wanda Jones, and Yolanda Paden-Brown, Yolanda Singletary, Yolanda Wright, and Yvonne Butler.

Thank you to all of you for allowing me to connect with that special part of you and for accepting, supporting and celebrating me as I accepted, supported and celebrated you. Loving you helped me to love myself!

Table of Contents

✳

Foreword

By Bishop Matthew E. Bradby, II

*L*et me first say that I have read this book as a man and I found it a joy and an honor to do so! It was the first book I ever read that presented a diagram for life, the process of life and real tools to handle the problem both as an individual and as a team. Thank you for writing this MASTERPIECE! Below is the forward God blessed me to write on your behalf.

There are times in life when you take a gamble and years later, you must agree it was well worth the risk. That gamble for me was to continue pastoring a small church in east Baltimore even when no one was sitting in the seats. It was in this humility that I laid ground for a true legacy. In that legacy, great people of power and faith have come to the ministry bringing great experiences, gifting, vision and blessings. Today as I sit back marveling at the masterpiece sitting before you, I can truly say, I know this great woman of transparency and the story within these pages. Through God's guidance

I have watched this woman grow from a seedling to a powerful redwood in a matter of months. I have relied on her keen sense of judgment, wisdom and expertise in areas that many of her superiors could not be entrusted.

It takes great pressure to produce a diamond. I am glad to find such a gem in Cheryle T. Ricks. It is my prayer and request that every woman share this great work with another woman. I pray that every father gives a copy of this masterpiece to his daughters! That every husband shares this literary work with their wives and every friend finds a woman in their life and let this book bloom the flower of life in her that only a woman like Cheryle can, through the truth of her life. Every woman needs a circle of sisters. Every woman needs healing. Every woman needs identity of self and true wholeness. Every woman must undertake the journey of wholeness for herself.

I believe from the bottom of my heart that if the biblical character, Tamar, (who had been raped by her brother Amnon in 2 Samuel 13) had this wealth of wisdom and a woman like a Cheryle T. Ricks and her sister circle mentioned in this masterpiece, she would not have led a desolate life, but could have been re-born as a rose in the midst of thorns.

So, in conclusion, great women of power and faith, women of every color, creed, nationality and economical status, it is to you I salute, as you are embarking on a journey to refine (not just re-define) yourselves. This journey will be one of great honesty, integrity, pain, promise and power. For many, you have done the impossible by just picking up this book to read it. To others it is the fact that you now realize you are bigger and much better than what you have experienced. For a few, it will be the guide to hone your skills and make sense of the madness you are in the midst of.

In order to win, you must first acknowledge the race! In order to win the race, you must first make up in your mind that you will enter the contest with a mind to finish. My sister, as I finish, I salute you with these powerful words from William Shakespeare's *Hamlet* Act 1 Scene III "To thy ownself be true." It will not be easy, but you so deserve it. And so do the millions of female generations in line who need a conclusion to the mysteries of womanhood and the bond that all women share.

- Bishop Matthew E. Bradby, II

Introduction

❋

"Life Is A Bud Waiting To Blossom"

Like a bud on a bare tree waiting anxiously
for the awakening of spring. Counting
the time it will be with each day closer
to spring. Anticipating it's true self and
what life will be. Time is here, for it is
spring. It blooms into a flower. Beautiful
to See, Beautiful to Be!

- Cheryle T. Ricks

Have you ever asked yourself, why you don't get
along with other women or why you are always
getting hurt and feeling so badly about yourself? Have you
ever tried to figure out why being a woman is so hard and it
doesn't matter what you do; you keep coming back to the
same place with the same pain? Have you ever wondered
why some women seem to have it all together when your
life seems to be getting more and more miserable? Well,
you are not alone. The book you are holding will answer

these questions and a whole lot more. It will help you find yourself and teach you how to love the you that you find. It will help you process all of those things that brought you so much pain by identifying what the womanhood process is and how to complete it. It will allow you to see that the very thing we need as women is the very thing we avoid, each other.

The key to our well-being is in the hands of the women in our circle. Over the years, women have distanced themselves from one another and some women now view each other as enemies. However, our strength and wholeness comes from interacting with other women. We have a great deal in common because of the process of womanhood. It is the same for all women. It plays out in different ways, but the pits we all fall into bring the same pain and devaluation to each of us. When women mature enough to recognize that other women are allies and not enemies; we gain the true secret of womanhood, oneness. God created the world, but women nurture it. God has entrusted women with this awesome job because He has connected us to the universe. Women have the ability to identify what is going on and what is needed. Therefore, we have our hand on the pulse of everything. What an honor and privilege to be chosen as the keepers of the world. But this job is too great for any of us to do on our own. We need each other! Together we stand, divided we all fall, along with everyone who is depending on us! You can have a life that you enjoy waking up to even if you are facing a problem or difficult situation by allowing God to love you right where you are, the way you are. Also, by learning that receiving forgiveness and giving forgiveness frees us from the prison that many of us find ourselves in. We must give ourselves permission to be human and imperfect while still having a right relationship with ourselves, which is the key to having a right relationship with others. A sister circle will do just that, because it is a group of women who come together for the purpose of sharing their frustrations, challenges and fears; to gain the knowledge, assistance, help and support that will equip them to become better mothers, grandmothers, daughters, sisters, aunts, friends, and wives to their families and community. A sister circle can help women to understand their value, worth and their importance to the betterment of our world.

After many years ministering and talking to women from different stages of life, I have discovered that many of them are facing some of the same issues that hinder them from enjoying their lives. In this book, I hope to identify some of those issues and provide solutions that will enable each woman to see the realities that are not so evident in their busy lives and allow them to finally process the hurt that many women are currently dealing with. So, come with me on this journey and discover the answer to that question: How can I have the life that I truly desire?

PART I:

The Way We Are

Chapter One

The Heart Of A Woman

✳

CARES ABOUT EVERYONE

*W*omen naturally love. We are compassionate towards others and we feel their pain. We sometimes transfer their pain to ourselves. Women feel everything deeply. Because of this, we try to do everything we can to stop others from hurting. We remember so well how our own pain felt and what we went through that we don't want anyone else to hurt. We will even hurt ourselves rather than allow someone else to be hurt. We tell ourselves; "I can handle the pain a lot better than the person I care about." For some reason, we believe that others are unable to go through the trials of life that we did. Somehow we feel that others don't deserve to learn what only life can teach them. We don't want any of our love ones to suffer in anyway. Therefore, we endure hardships and heartbreaks to try to save them from the very thing they need; the full life experience.

Caring is part of what gives us the feeling of being needed. However, our need to save other people can cause more harm than good. We interfere with their development and we make them too dependent on us. When we die or end the relationship, they are unable to care for themselves because they never had the opportunity. This person becomes unable to make it in the big bad world and they can thank us for that. Let's face it; you have become who you are by learning from and enduring the trials of life. You made it and you are better able to help others make it too if you let them take their own steps. They will thank you for the journey.

GIVES HER WHOLE SELF

Women give all or nothing. When we see a need or someone needs help, we do any and everything to meet that need. Because we have the gift of hope, we find a way to get that done. We are the creative source that can make a way when it looks like there is no way, because we are connected to God in a very special way. We can pray and cry out to God for whatever is needed. Women have a special place in the heart of God. However, women can sometimes give their lives by giving up on life all together.

Women become a part of what we give ourselves to. We have a hard time disconnecting ourselves from what we do and it causes us to forget our value and worth. Sometimes life just doesn't turn out the way we planned it and many of us are unable to bounce back from situations that have consumed us. We internalize what we go through and we make ourselves out as "the bad girl", blaming ourselves for anything that went wrong or for the way others have mistreated us. Because of this, we start the downward spiral to self-hate. We fail to find anything good in ourselves. We talk negative to and about ourselves because of what has happened to us. Some women spend years making other people's lives miserable because they no longer want to have a relationship with themselves. We can never hope to have a good relationship with others without first having a good relationship with ourselves. We can only have a right relationship with ourselves by first having a right relationship with God. He created us and only He knows who we truly are. When life becomes too difficult to handle, look to those people in your circle who genuinely love and care about you, the real you, not the person you think you are when you mess-up. They will help you see that you are not the mistakes you make and that you can get pass what you are going through. They will show you how to work through the pain and position yourself for a new beginning.

LONG SUFFERING

The heart of a woman has the ability to suffer a long time. Women endure pain from our lovers, friends, bosses, and co-workers, but one of the greatest pains a woman can feel comes from her children. We give them the best we have, but it is never enough. Our children are the only people with the power to stab us in our heart and leave us the walking dead. Their words cut deeper than any knife! Their ungratefulness is a punch in the face that makes us feel like a fool. That pain is greatest when we watch our children being disrespected and abused by others. We watch those same children give their abusers forgiveness after forgiveness and chance after chance only to receive more of the same mistreatment. A woman doesn't stop doing for her children. Even though her children make it perfectly clear that they do not want her in their lives or the lives of their children. We learn to accept our children's rejection and take the pain to God who heals our heart and gives us a brand new start. We even learn to love other people's children who wish that they had a mother just like us. I loved my mother, but I never understood why she would love and nurture us and did nothing to obtain her own happiness. In the end, she died an unfulfilled woman. No one is perfect and all of us are doing the best we know to do. Stop punishing yourself for what you didn't do. We cannot go back in time and change the past. Wherever you are in life, you can only do what you know to do at that time. The best thing we can do is to learn as we go, do what we know and seek knowledge and wisdom from God to help guide us. For everything that did not go the way you wished it had, give it to God and let Him heal it and fill it with His love. Live your life with God as your focus and you will discover a place that brings joy and wholeness.

COMMITS FOR LIFE

Women have a "never say die attitude." We never give up. When we do, it is because we have given all that we had and it was not enough. We endure one relationship after another because we are committed. We sign up for the long haul. In our mind, every problem has a solution and we know that we can find it. However, the solution we find requires the assistance of others before it can work. In most cases, that other person does not want to do their part. Therefore, we look for other solutions that we feel we can do on our own, only to find that we are the only person who wants to solve the problem. A problem for us is not a problem for the person that we are in relationship with, because they are getting what they want at our expense. Therefore, the other person offers no help. This type of relationship usually involves a giver and a taker; someone giving their whole heart and someone who gives very little, if at all. Commitment is necessary for every achievement. However, sometimes the thing that we are committed to is the very thing that is causing the pain and heartache we are feeling. When a relationship ends, it is not always a bad thing. Life is full of seasons and every season has a reason. Trying to make a season when there is no reason is pointless and unproductive. However, because most of us do not take the time to assess the relationships that we are in, we hold onto relationships that no longer give us what we need. Those relationships also stop us from knowing the person we are today. Stop trying to fit the new you into relationships made for the person you used to be. This process is called growing up and evolving. Staying with people you have outgrown will only cause you to regress and will hinder you from becoming the person God has created you to be. Allow God to bring new people in your life who will appreciate you for who you are today and help you to see the growth and wisdom that makes you a person anyone would love to know.

NURTURES EVERYTHING SHE TOUCHES

Like her womb; a woman is a gift of life, not just in childbirth, but in everything she touches. In her lies the key that unlocks the potential within others. Women give all that they have to see that potential manifest in others. When people fail to believe in themselves, she will believe for them until they can. When women stop nurturing, it is because our heart is broken and the pain outweighs our hope. Therefore, we have to guard our hearts—guard them, not lock them up. Just as our heart can hurt us, it is also the one thing that makes us unique.

A woman with no heart is not a woman at all; her heart is what makes her a woman. Her heart is what connects her to God, and the only thing that enables her to do all the things that she does. This explains why women die when they stop loving. They disconnect from their source and become unable to do what they were created to do, and the life within them dies.

Women are energy sources to others, and others are an energy source to them. That's why women have to remember to stay connected to each other. No woman is an island unto herself. Therefore, we must never retreat to ourselves too long, because we become defeated when we are by ourselves. The devil gets in our heads and fills us with doubt and hopelessness as we look continually at our situation and not to the God of our hope. Isolation is the biggest pit for women because we punish and blame ourselves when we are there. This is because we are absent from the support and encouragement that we need all the time. A woman without support is like a fish out of water. We will not last very long without the presence of others.

God designed us to be interconnected. We are to work together and help each other recognize our value and worth. Most of us devalue ourselves while valuing everyone else. The problem is that we give so much of ourselves without allowing others to give to us. We sometimes have a false sense of giving. We often reject the blessings that others offer us. When others try to show us appreciation, we say; "That's alright, I didn't do it for that." Later, we become resentful that others are getting so much from us and no one is giving anything to us. From there, we go to "it's all about me," but there is no balance in that.

When we learn to include ourselves while caring for others, we find the true meaning of caring. However, we cannot expect others to do for us what we won't do for ourselves. Learn to do things that you enjoy. Take some time on a regular basis to rejuvenate yourself. Surround yourself with people who give and receive. Stop all relationships with takers, and you will enjoy your life in a more fulfilling way.

FAITH TO BELIEVE

A woman's faith is what activates her power to love. In her mind, love will make everything better, and it will. Women believe that things can be a lot better than they appear at this moment. She becomes a source of hope for everyone who comes to her for help. God has brought her through so many trials that she can walk with others when they are in their dark places. She understands that morning will come. However, she can spend so much time being all things to all people that she fails to have faith in herself and the plan God has for her life. She encourages others with the word of God, but forgets that those same words apply to her. Therefore, it is important that women make time for God and fellowship with other people who are spiritually stronger than we are. When we allow time for our own spiritual growth, we are able to minister healing to others. We can do this by listening and talking to people who are spiritually grounded. They show us how to live our lives with a lot less fear and uncertainty by helping us realize that everything in the natural started in the spirit. That knowledge keeps us calm when life just doesn't go the way we want it to. Putting our faith in God allows us to become everything He created us to be and our lives will become purposeful and more meaningful. Faith is the one thing that makes life doable. Therefore, building our faith is one of the best things we can do to bring out the best in our lives. When our faith grows, we will be better able to walk in the faith that God has given to us while helping others walk in theirs.

Chapter Two

The Depth Of Her Love

✳

PATIENT TO A FAULT

*W*omen can wait and wait and wait some more, because we know what the end can be. We do the same thing day in and day out, year after year, delay after delay, set back after set back. We keep on watching and working until that thing comes to pass. We wait for our man to stop doing that destructive thing. We wait for that child to finally understand the lessons that we have been trying to teach him, or that friend to finally see that she is better than she allows her man to treat her. Patience is a virtue and the key to the best in life. Because women can see what others cannot, we continue to wait and pray with expectancy. We can walk through the process with others, but we don't give that same time and energy to our own process. We are too tired or we just don't feel that we are worth all the work, even though we gladly do it for others. In most cases, we do most of the work for them. The biggest challenge we face as women is that we don't understand how valuable we are. To us, we are just us. None of us are special to ourselves, but we are very special to each other. We bring something to others that can only be given if we give it. As my friend, Cathy helped me to see; we were not made to help ourselves, but to help others and allow others to help us. When we share our unique gifts and abilities, we enhance one another, which make a better world for all of us. Everyone is needed and everyone matters. Therefore, tell the women in your circle how important they are to you and how much you appreciate them and let them do the same thing for you. Then live your life in such a way that the world will remember that you were here!

DEPENDABILITY IS WHO SHE IS

Women are some of the most loyal people on the planet. We will support you in any way we can. We will go out of our way to prove that we are a friend for life. We will baby sit your children to give you some rest. We will sit with your sick parent for months at a time to let you know that you are not in it alone. We will come to your paint party even though we don't really know how to paint. We take great joy in doing whatever is needed. We were created to make a difference, and we do the moment we get out of bed. Women are energy sources. We bring a special kind of something to the world. We can cheer someone up by giving them a hug, an encouraging word or just a smile. We are great givers. However, most of us don't know how to receive the good, because we were never taught how. For years, we watched our mothers and grandmothers give and never receive. We are quick to say; "What goes around comes around." However, we only believe that the bad things we do are coming back. The truth is we don't believe that the good we do will come back to us just as easily. Therefore, we never get the things we desire. We can only get what we believe we can have. Many of us have unfulfilled lives because we don't believe that our lives can be any more than what it is at this moment. Determine in yourself today that you will receive a harvest from all the good seeds you have sown throughout your life. Then get ready for the overflowing blessings that you desire and allow God to use you in a greater way.

HER THRESHOLD OF PAIN

The pain that women can endure can only be compared to labor pains. Women give birth to lots of things. Our vision for others is so sharp and on point that we can plan a course to bring it to life. However, we cannot see the vision for our own lives. We often disqualify ourselves from a life that we can readily see for others. Many of us live our lives in the past. The pain from the past keeps us from moving forward. We are unable to break free. We are full of shame for what others have done to us. We also blame ourselves for those things that we have done or for things that were not in our power to do. When we relive pass hurts, it hinders us from seeing that the future can be full of happiness. Everyday, we relive the things that others have done to us. We refuse to let them off the hook. We never plan to forgive them. We think that we are punishing them. We do not realize that they have gone on with their lives and the only person that's suffering is ourselves. Unforgiveness is a prison we put ourselves in. The funny thing is that we have the only key to our prison door. The pain we feel has convinced us that the person who hurt us, is hurting too. When the truth is, the moment we forgive someone is the same moment the healing starts in our hearts. Unforgiveness poisons our heart and stops the flow of love which means that our lives begin to decay. It will continue to do so until it eats us alive. Therefore, take this time to forgive anyone that has ever hurt you, and give your pain to God.

Take this time to also forgive yourself. I repeat, none of us is perfect and all of us are doing the best we know to do. So stop punishing yourself for what you didn't do. We cannot go back in time and change the past. Wherever you are in life, you can only do what you know to do at that time. The best thing we can do is to learn as we go and do what we know, and by seeking knowledge and wisdom from God to help guide us. For everything that did not go the way you wished it had, give it to God and let Him heal it and fill it with His love. Again, making God the most important person in your life brings you everything you need to fill the emptiness in your soul. Let God's love heal you and restore you to wholeness so that you are ready to receive the love God has just for you!

As women, we need to release one another. Many of our mothers and sisters have not gone through the womanhood process successfully and because of this they were not able to help us with our journey. This explains why we have gone through so much pain. As a daughter; forgive your mother for what she did not give you, whether she had it to give or not. Just like you, your mother was going through some of the same things that you are. If you are a mother, your children are likely lacking some of the things they need from you too. Life can be hard and the weight of our pain can take our minds away from the people we love the most. Forgive your sisters. As young women, we were all in desperate need of approval and acceptance. Most of us had a poor self image that made us feel inadequate. Many of us were secretly abused and mistreated, therefore we hurt one another. The pain that we are dealing with can only be healed when we forgive the women that have caused the pain. That pain has put us in a prison and we have served our sentence many times over. Therefore, I am asking that each of you allow the women that have hurt you to be given parole because none of us can go back and do anything over, but we can resolve those things that keep causing the pain. Let us agree to start over and go forward, leaving the past in the past by redefining the relationship we want today. Ask each other for the forgiveness you both desperately need. Then identify the needs you both have today. Let each other know how you want the other to relate as the relationship moves forward. Give each other a hug and let the love flow again! Then learn to appreciate the growth in one another and enjoy the relationship you finally have with each other.

SACRIFICING IS A LIFESTYLE

Women are very good at sacrificing themselves for the people they love. There is no limit to what a woman will give up for someone she cares about. Sometimes it is out of loyalty and obligation. Nevertheless, she gives all that she has to meet their need. I have witnessed several grandmothers raising their grandchildren in their fifties, sixties and older. They have decided to forgo their senior years to do anything that will keep their families together. Many of them are very sickly and are not fully equipped to parent at that season of life. Nonetheless, they are determined that they will do what ever it takes and they sometimes pay the ultimate price, their life. I have also observed those same children disrespecting those grandmothers. Those children make their grand-mothers feel like they are doing the grandmothers a favor by allowing their grandmothers to care for them. I have even seen women take their parents out of nursing homes who required 24-hour care. I have seen those same women almost die themselves trying to do what requires more than one person to do. I have watched women work two and three jobs to give their children the very best that there is. The more they gave, the more they needed to give. I have also seen women give their jobs so much of themselves that they had no life to live. They even refused to take time for doctor appointments or vacations. When they finally did retire, they did not live too long afterwards because they never took the time to care about their own health.

Sacrificing one's life is admirable. However, too often it ends with very little benefit for the person who makes the sacrifice. When will women learn that it is better to help where we can and do only those things that we are able to do and allow others to do the rest? This will allow us to truly enjoy every season of our lives. We just need to say, "I can help with this part of the problem." This frees us from taking on someone else's burdens, and allows others to do all that they can to help themselves so they will experience a sense of responsibility and self-worth. Then we will be better able to do so much more of the things we desire as we include ourselves in the equation; do for others and include ourselves. Women would give better care to others if they would permit others to give them the help they need. Then we will be able to pass the torch to the next generation by teaching others how to do all of the things that we do. This is our legacy.

Chapter Three

The Enemy In Me

❋

SAVING YOU AND KILLING ME

As women, we give until we can give no more. Then we are empty of strength, tired from lack of rest, feeling devalued and unappreciated for all the things we do. The price we pay for the love that we desire is greater than we can afford. Yet, we keep giving until it takes our breath, our health or completely breaks our spirit. We feel alone and have nowhere to turn for support. Instead, we look for love in all the wrong places from all the wrong people. I watch women everyday taking care of other people while hurting themselves. They all say the same thing; "I have to do what I have to do." I am so tired of seeing women value everything and everybody and completely devalue themselves. Every time I hear a woman say those words my heart breaks all over again. You see, my mother was a housewife for 35 years and she lived for her kids, my father, and her grandchildren. She never did anything for herself. She never fulfilled any of her dreams. She devoted her life to others. Her health was not an important matter to her. Her unhappiness did not help the high blood pressure she suffered with. She would get depressed and drink until she was drunk to cover the pain and emptiness she was feeling. She was sober more than she was drunk, but the tears she cried while she was drunk made me want to help her find some happiness. I would do her hair and listen when she talked about getting a job and leaving my father. My mother did not get a job, but she did leave my father and us, too. One day, my mother told us that she was having chest pains and we told her to go to the doctor and she said; "I'll be okay. I'll rest." Well, she is still resting. She had a massive heart attack a couple of days later and died! Now I am a motherless child because my mother couldn't love herself half as much as she loved me. I don't want to see another woman give her life so needlessly while saving so many others. I loved my mother, but I never understood why she would love and nurture us and did nothing to obtain her own happiness. In the end, she died an unfulfilled woman.

If helping me hurts you, please don't help me! If you want me to help you and you know that it will hurt me, I can't help you because the relationship is all about you and you don't really care about me. Therefore, I no longer want your relationship. As women, we allow people to bring us their problems to fix, but who can we bring all of our problems to and expect them to solve them, except God Himself? So why do we feel compelled to make other people's problems ours? Women would have a more fulfilled life with a lot less stress if we didn't help others based solely on our emotions and trying to be the hero. Let us allow God to guide us in how and when to help. This way we direct people to God and they will be able to get the best help possible.

EVERY ONE IS VALUABLE, BUT ME

As women, we have no idea how valuable we are. The people around us do, but they keep that knowledge from us so that they can continue to use us. Most of us see ourselves as very ordinary and fail to see how special we truly are. We do not understand that the things we do are essential to the people around us. We give our services to others for free or for a very small cost. Yet, we are happy to pay the best price for other people's services. This is one reason why so many of us struggle in our finances. We discount ourselves and rarely accept money for the services that we provide to others, who benefit in a major way. Women have the ability to earn a great deal of money. Instead, many of us are happy to work for others and make just enough to meet our needs. We are capable of working long hours in the home and on the job. If women were paid for all the jobs we perform on a regular basis, we would be wealthy. Many of us disqualify ourselves from having the best that we can. We motivate and inspire others to greatness, but somehow we have a very hard time encouraging ourselves to pursue our own dreams. We readily see that others have what it takes. However, we are unable to see that we do too.

One thing I noticed about women is that we cannot work as hard for ourselves as we work for our employers. When our boss tells us what he wants done, we have no problem organizing and producing a great product. We even give long hours and we do it sometimes while we are going through life challenges or sick and in pain. Somehow we don't have the same drive and devotion to making our own dreams come true. Many of us just can't seem to value ourselves enough to do what is in our best interest. As working women, we make our employers billions of dollars. Our dedication keeps those companies in business. This is why the sister circle is so important. It empowers and esteems each of us. We also learn how to launch out and make our dreams a reality by giving the support, resources and assistance that is needed. As someone once said, "We don't need to know everything. Just know the people who do." Together, we help each other spread our wings and give God all the glory that He desires from all of us.

RELATIONSHIPS ARE KEY

It doesn't matter who you are. It is your relationships that make your life. The problem is that many of us are in unhealthy relationships. Because of this, we live unfulfilled lives. As women, we can get so wrapped up in doing what we do so naturally, that we don't realize that we are being taken advantage of. Some of our relationships offer us no benefits. We have people in our lives that only take up space and weigh us down. Most often, we do not realize that we are the ones keeping the relationship going. We are the ones calling to check on our "friends." We are the ones giving our resources and time. However, we finally get a clue when we call those same "friends" when we are in need and find no help at all. We can not believe that some people are only in our lives for what they can get from us. So we soon start another unhealthy relationship and that relationship ends up the same way the last one did. The pain becomes so bad that we become a loner. We tell ourselves that everyone is like this. Many of us want people to give us things that they don't have to give or they just don't want to give to us. However, there are people around us that have something to give and are willing to give to us, but we don't want it from them. We want it from the people that we have invested much of our energy, resources, and time into. We don't seem to notice that we are the common denominator in all of our relationships.

I have learned that we draw people in our lives that treat us the same way they see us treat ourselves, which is why it is very important to have a healthy relationship with oneself before trying to have a relationship with others. If we don't like who we are, we will be insecure and lack the confidence that healthy relationships require. People will have to keep us fixed by trying to convince us that we are good enough to be with. This kind of relationship always leaves the insecure person feeling more unworthy and it causes them to have a poor self image.

Healthy relationships do not involve very needy people. They consist of two people who meet the needs of each other, both giving and receiving. If we don't have a healthy opinion of ourselves, people will come in our lives and abuse us. It is very important to understand your value and worth. However, that takes being around people who appreciate you and not just tolerate you. You cannot get appreciation from people who are envious of you and who secretly wish to be you. As women, we often expect others to give us what we should be giving ourselves or what we are unwilling to do for ourselves. I have heard many women say "when I get married my husband is going to do this and that for me. He is going to make me happy." When I ask those same women if they are doing any of those things for themselves, they all say "that is my husband's job". Please know that if we don't care enough about ourselves to do those things to make us happy, no one else will be willing to either. No one is responsible for our happiness. That is our own personal responsibility. If we are going to be happy, we must first make a conscious decision that we are going to be happy. Then we need to do those things that bring us happiness and stop doing those things that don't. Many of us expect others to know what makes us happy.

However, when someone asks us what makes us happy, we do not have a clue.

Therefore, as women we need to take some time to get to know ourselves and reconnect with those things that bring joy to us by spending some time on a regular basis discovering who we are today. You would be amazed to find that you are a brand new person with different needs than you did five or ten years ago. Because of this you could find yourself living with a stranger. We need to stay in touch with ourselves. I realize that we are all busy with life and all of our responsibilities, but spending some quality time alone with yourself is the most valuable thing you can do to ensure that your life is on course and purposeful. It will help you with all of your other relationships in a major way. When we are in a relationship with someone, we want them to meet our needs without knowing what our needs are. I find that taking a bath at the end of the day instead of a shower gives me time to reflect and reassess my life and my relationships. It is also a great way to transition from work to home. The bathroom is the only place where others will leave us to ourselves. When we learn to have healthy relationships with ourselves, it has a positive effect on all of our relationships, especially with other women and with our children. We are then able to help our daughters become better equipped to be women. We can also help our daughters avoid some of the pain that we had to endure.

Many of the issues we are facing today started when we were very young. Those life-changing experiences have caused many of us to become stuck. Because of this, we missed some developmental steps along the way.

Therefore, things that we should have learned at different stages of our lives, we did not. As women, many of us had to grow up too fast. We missed being a little girl and many of our teen years were spent dealing with adult issues. Now that we are "grown" there are unresolved issues in our lives.

However, because many of us have not built a healthy relationship with ourselves, we have not processed our pain. People we trusted hurt us or neglected us in some way and that pain is still hindering us from having healthy relationships today. Because we are not whole, we stay in relationships that are very harmful. Therefore, we are causing our daughters and sons to live in that same pain. Our unsolved pain affects our children and causes them to feel disconnected. It also makes them feel inadequate. Our children look to us for sound advice, nurturing and love but we are unable to provide it because our problems and our pain have become our constant companion. They need a relationship with us and we give them stuff. They come to us for guidance and direction and we give them neither. It is no wonder that young children think about killing themselves.

Often times, we do not see our relationships realistically. We often look at them based on what we want them to be or what they have the potential of becoming, or how they can be if certain things were to change in our relationships. However, this is not how relationships become healthy. When women can see their mates for who they are and respect the way they see themselves, we can build relationships that will be fruitful and enjoyable. The other person has to work on his character development and actively take steps towards the vision for his life. Some of us are in relationships that we never intended to be in. We started going out with a man and the next thing we knew we were a couple. We never assessed the person to see if he could meet our needs or if he met any of the requirements needed for a healthy relationship. Because he took us out and wanted to be with us we thought it could be a beneficial relationship. However, we later learned that he did not have any of the things needed to build a good relationship. He was just someone to hang out with. We then spend years with him, only to receive none of what we need in a mate. One reason for this is that most of us don't like to be by ourselves. Someone has convinced us that if we are alone, we are also lonely and that could not be further from the truth. You can be in a room full of people and still be lonely. You can also be in a relationship and be alone.

Again, healthy relationships start with having one with yourself; that takes spending some time with yourself, being single and not romantically involved with anyone. For many of us, our self image comes from having a man and being viewed as sexy. However, when we like who we are, we are confident and this makes us truly sexy. **Because we know our value and worth we are happy even if we are not in a relationship with a man. In fact, our men friends find us very attractive and sexy. Those men learn that there is so much more to enjoy with a woman who doesn't feel that she is only good for sexual pleasure. He learns that she is a person and not just a sex toy. Men who truly value women have a greater level of respect for all women. He does not cross the line romantically. The truth be told, most of our relationships are formed and** maintained with sex and there is an emptiness that comes with this kind of relationship. Many women believe that they need to have a sexual relationship with a man when many of us really just want the male presence in our lives. We want his companionship and we want to hear his deep voice, see his muscular body, feel his strength, and experience real safety. As we understand our value and worth, we learn how to truly appreciate the relationships we have with all the men in our lives. We learn that having a good relationship with ourselves also enables us to complete the healing process.

After we have processed the pain in our lives, we can then appreciate the blessing of a whole man, a man who has processed the pain in his own life. A whole man is God's greatest gift to women. However, we have to learn to value that gift. A man covers us and looks out for our best interest. He takes away a lot of the worries we had when we were single. Therefore, we no longer have to carry the load of life on our shoulders. God has entrusted men to care for us. A man can truly care for us when he lets God help him be all the man that he can be. He is able to guide us because he allows God to guide him. God designed men and women to work together and complement each other. A man is a woman's protector, provider and, strength. A woman is a man's support, helper, and encourager. When a man finally finds the woman that God has created just for him, he is now in his proper place. He now has purpose and fulfillment. God created men to take care of his family. Everything that a man does in life leads to taking care of everything that

God has created. Therefore, we must learn to respect the men God has put in our lives and honor them. A whole man will fight for his family everyday of his life as long as he has a woman who appreciates and celebrates him for doing it. So learn the men in your life and what honors them. Give them the respect that God asks us to give them and together we will bring the glory back to God!

PART II

The Way We Were Created To Be

Chapter Four

Our Beauty Is Within Us

GOD'S GARDEN OF FLOWERS

*A*s women, our beauty is within and it cannot be compared to anyone else's. We are more beautiful than we can imagine. However, when we look at ourselves, we can only see our flaws and imperfections. We remember all of the negative things that people have said about us. Some of us believe that we look like the awful things that have been done to us. If we can focus on the positive things about ourselves, we will see ourselves like a flower in a garden. How beautiful the garden of women who flower the earth? We are all beautiful flowers in God's garden. No flower is any lovelier than the other. When we look at a garden of flowers, we admire the whole garden and every flower we see. We don't hear the flowers saying I'm not beautiful because that flower looks more beautiful than me. As women, we are all one of a kind and very rare. I cannot bring to the world what only you can and you cannot bring to the world what only I can, but if I don't give my part and you don't give your part, the world will be without that very necessary something that makes the world work. So stop comparing and judging yourself based on what other women are, or what they are not. You are the only you there is and if you concentrate on being the best you, you will find the beauty that is within you! So go out and let your beauty shine forth and be the blessing that God made you to be!

SHOW ME THE ME YOU SEE

As women, many of us have a distorted view of ourselves. When women are asked to tell something about themselves, they talk about the roles they play. We tend to define ourselves by our jobs or titles. Many of us do not have a good sense of self. When we look outside of ourselves for what can only be found within us, we hit one brick wall after another. We cannot find our identity and value in our clothes, make-up, things or in other people. God is the master creator and He has put everything women need inside of us, the problem is that we cannot see it on our own. God made women so special that He does not allow us to see what only others can. Therefore, when we are alone, without other positive people in our lives, we are only able to see the things we don't like and not the things that make us so special. When most of us look at ourselves, we can only see our flaws and none of the other wonderful qualities that only come to surface when we interact with others. Remember that women are givers and it is in our giving that the true us comes out. Therefore, when we include other women in our circle, it helps each of us become our best. We learn that being transparent will allow us and the women around us to understand our purpose and the true meaning of life.

Therefore, it is very important to surround yourself with people who are secure enough in themselves to give you a list of all the wonderful qualities and abilities that they see in you. Many of them would tell you that you are giving, helpful, talented in several areas, and that you have been there for them when they were going through some very hard times, to name just a few. Just like you, there are women around you who need your eyes to see their wonderful qualities. So every time you encounter a woman, tell her something that you see in her that she cannot see herself. It will make a world of difference to her and it will help you appreciate yourself as well.

MY ANSWERS ARE IN YOU

The enemy has convinced us that other women are not to be trusted, and that we are trying to take each other's man or we are trying to stab each other in the back. However, this is a lie from the pit of Hell. The truth is, that each woman holds the key to one of the problems that another woman is struggling with. However, the best way to keep women in the pits we fall into is by keeping us apart and isolated from one another. The victories that women have achieved are pathways that will lead other women out of the situations that they are facing.

How many women throughout the world have overcome many of the same challenges that many women are dealing with today? The problem is that we cannot obtain the knowledge and insight that will deliver us because it is in the hands of the women around us. If we continue to view other women as a threat or as an enemy, we will stay in the place of our pain. I have been through domestic violence, having children without being married, an abortion, a mental breakdown and no self-esteem, to mention just a few, and I have gotten the victory in each of these areas. However, I am not the only one. There are many other women who have been through these same situations, and much more. Therefore, each of us holds the key to the problem that is keeping another woman up at night and causing her to feel that she cannot overcome it. Think about this, if you were traveling to another city, wouldn't it be wonderful if you were traveling with someone who lives in that city, someone who knows all the back roads and the ideal time to start the trip? That is the exact thing you get when you connect with other women who have gone through what you are going through. They can tell you how to get on the other side of what's destroying your life. They can also walk with you and hold your hand so you are not alone.

There are women in our lives that we admire, who represent the qualities that tell us that they are over-comers. Reach out to one of them and tap into the wisdom and knowledge that she has. It will enable you to start a brand new life. Remember she too, is a woman who loves to feel needed. She would also love to see her fellow sister stand up and be all God has created her to be.

I NEED YOU TO VALIDATE ME

As women, we look to anyone and everything for validation except to the only person who can give it. A woman's true validation can only come from other women. Only other women can give us the approval that lets us know that we are a good representation of womanhood. However, many of us try to get our validation from men and it has caused some of us to be abused or mistreated. The right kind of validation that men can give is to help us feel secure as their ladies by showing us appreciation for what we bring to their lives and recognizing that we are a valuable part of their world. When we are trying to figure out how to be a woman, another woman who has a good grasp on womanhood can point us into the right direction.

As a mother of twin daughters, I felt compelled to validate them on their 30th birthday, so I wrote them a poem entitled "When A Woman Turns 3O". In that poem, I told them all the qualities that I saw in them and all the wonderful things that they were now capable of doing. I told them that they were on target as women. I also told them that they were now ready to make their dreams come true. I told them how proud I was of them and that I loved them very much. On that same birthday, I took them to dinner and I gave each of them a $50.00 bill. However, they stated that the words in the poem meant more to them than the meal or the money.

As women, we do so many things and we do them the best we can. How nice it is when our peers tell us we are doing a good job. You cannot put a price tag on the words. Let us help one another feel that security and support that affirms how valuable and special we are. Therefore, when you are in the presence of other women, give them their pats on the back and tell them something that will lift their spirit and self-esteem. Let them know that they are doing a good job. We need each other more than you can begin to imagine. Many of us are being mistreated and made to feel worthless. Therefore, we need someone to speak life into us and remind us that the things we are dealing with will get better. A lot of the women we see everyday are looking for hope and a way out of the situations they are going through. Let each of us be that hope to one another!

HELP! I'VE FALLEN AND I CAN'T GET UP

Women all over the world have been in or are currently in a state of despair. Some are at their wits end and if God doesn't do something they will not be able to hold on. Their pain and the heaviness of their situation seem too much to bear. As women, we go through so many hardships and heartbreaks. However, several of them could have been avoided. The problem is that many women are trying to be a woman without having relationships with other women. We must realize that the womanhood process is not something that can be done alone. Traveling this road called womanhood is full of pits that can cause us very serious harm that can take years to overcome. The sister circle is a place to help each other get through life without having to endure the worse possible hardships. When women connect with one another, we become the guiding light that directs us away from trouble.

When we find ourselves in a difficult situation and we don't know what to do, we must first admit that we are in a place that we cannot fix ourselves. Then we need to call on God to help us and He will put someone in our path that we can trust. That person will listen to us as we tell them what we are struggling with. They will help us see the problem from a different perspective. It is difficult to see the whole problem because we are too close to it. We truly "cannot see the forest for the trees."

There is something special when one woman takes the time to walk with another woman who is going through a tough place. The comfort the hurting woman receives is so wonderful. They are not concerned about their looks or their image. They have united to do what God has equipped them to do as women. God has given us the strength to get through every challenge we are facing. The bonding that takes place in women is what womanhood is all about. This kind of unity is available to every woman who learns who she is and why God has made her a woman. Again, if you have not experienced the support of other women, make it a goal to reach out to some mature women and experience the power of sisterhood. Then you can enjoy womanhood the way God designed it to be.

Chapter Five

The Strength In Our Pain

❄

THE SECRET TO WOMANHOOD

The secret to womanhood is to be what God created us to be, women of purpose, on a mission, working together in a unified way to nurture and care for the people He brings into our lives. However, women must first get away from meaningless conversations and doing unproductive things. Then we will find the purpose that fulfills us and gives us worth and value. Our worth and value is never based on what we have, where we live or if we have a man or not. However, women can find some of the worst things to try to get our value and validation from. We work so hard to be all things to all people. We sometimes lose ourselves in the process by pleasing everyone and never doing the things that give value to us. Then one day we wake up and we don't remember who we are. We say to ourselves, "I know I'm a mother, a daughter, a sister, a grandmother, a wife, a girlfriend, but who am I? The answer to that question is one of the solutions to all the problems we are facing. When we get in touch with who we are, and not by the roles we play, we find out who God says we are. We no longer define ourselves by what we have done or what has been done to us. We discover the true us, a woman of value and an instrument in the hands of God. We are a necessary part of God's plan for mankind. We no longer look at ourselves as sex objects, but God's gift to the world, who impacts every thing in the universe. Therefore, when you are having a day filled with negative thoughts about the person you are, remember God does everything through women. If there were no women in the world, the world would lose its meaning. Thinking about this will give you the hope you need to celebrate the person that God has made you.

YOUR PAIN CREATED THE REAL YOU

Life is the best mentor there is. The struggles we face and the hardships that we endure do a work in us like nothing else can. With every trial, we learn more about who we are and what we are made of. Often times, we are able to stand face to face with many challenges because we have evolved during our past trials. The fabric of a woman is brought to life as she is tried and tested. As painful as those trials were, it has taught us how to be much stronger. Because of this, we have become the women we are today. We were shaped by our times of brokenness. I have been through so many hard times that when I look at the person I use to be and then look at the person I am today, I can truly say that if I hadn't gone through all those bad times, I would not be the person I am today.

Today, I am a powerful woman that God uses to get things done in the Earth. I have the strength to face trials and tests that would have gotten the best of me years ago. My greatest victory was learning that I needed the wisdom of other women to help me on my journey. Now I have much more strength and knowledge to face life challenges because of my "sister circle." Therefore, give yourself the opportunity to be the best woman that you can be by reaching out to your fellow sisters all around the world. Share your story and insights with other women so that our world can become the place where every woman will experience the love that truly heals her brokenness.

HEALED AND READY FOR WAR

As women, we can go through life believing all kinds of lies that people have spoken over our lives. That is why having a sister circle is so important. Because of the pain we have endured, we can now help other women understand that their worth is not determined by what others say about them or the mistreatment that they have suffered. Our worth is determined by the strength that we discover inside of ourselves. For every victory, there is a process that we have to complete. Therefore, do not despise humble beginnings. Everyone's bad start has the ability to create an awesome finish.

When I was a young housewife, I was physically and verbally abused by my husband. I believed that I was ugly and I deserved the abuse I was receiving. After I got out of that relationship, others helped me to believe that I was pretty. However, when I tried to get a job, the people who interviewed me liked me, but they all asked me the same question, "what can you do?" I had no skills that anyone would pay me for. Therefore, I considered myself a pretty bum. Many years have passed since then and I now know the truth about who I really am. I learned the truth when I started my relationship with God through Jesus Christ. Today, I know that I am beautiful. According to God, I am also fearfully and wonderfully made. Because of my relationship with God, I am healed and whole. I was able to forgive my former husband and build a friendship with him that allowed us to co-parent our children. When we take the time and the steps to heal; life becomes grander than we could have ever imagined!

Now that each of us has overcome many of the challenges we faced, it is time to stand up and become a vessel that God can use to deliver other women around us. Let us celebrate the journey and the victory together.

Chapter Six

Lessons To Remember

❉

HOLD MY HAND AND DON'T LET ME GO

The sister circle has many advantages that each of us can enjoy. As women, we are ruled by our emotions and our need to nurture every thing and everyone. Often, we live our lives from the pain we are experiencing. Because of this, we don't always make the best decisions and choices. Wrong choices and bad decisions can cause a great deal of pain and throw our lives off course. Therefore, we need other women who are whole and healed to help us see those things that we are unable to see. They can advise us in those times when we are hurting emotionally and mentally out of it. They help us see situations and the people who come into our lives in a realistic way. There are also times in our lives when we are going through some very hard challenges and we just need a friend to go through it with us so we are not alone. That other sister is there to help care for the kids and assist with those things that must be done during those challenging times. She is there to cry with you, share your pain and comfort you while reassuring you that you are going to get through what you are dealing with. She is there to help you see that the guy you recently started dating is not everything he makes out to be and that you need to slow down before you get hurt again. She is there with you when you are celebrating the milestones in your life; like graduation, a new job, your wedding day, the birth of your children, and the day God makes one of your dreams come true, like writing a book. They are there to support you and encourage you and love you through all of the changes you go through in life. Their love is life giving and a real joy to share. Therefore, thank God for all of those wonderful sisters that have been there throughout your life.

THE MISSING PEACE

Life can be so difficult that it can become over-whelming. The weight and pressure of it all causes sleepless nights and stress filled days. You worry yourself into believing that you will not be able to get through what you are facing. Your mind is never at rest. You are barely able to keep yourself and the other people you are responsible for together. You are trying to sort out how to handle it all and depression starts to set in. I have been through times like that and God's peace was the only solution. True peace can only come from having a relationship with God.

Peace is the most priceless thing any of us can have because it allows us to stay calm even when we are dealing with the hardest times in life. God loves us so much that He allows us to take all of our problems, worries, concerns, fear, and our hopes and dreams to Him. God tells us to cast all of our concerns on Him because He cares for us. God gives us the ability to manage the things that we cannot without Him. God has a way of making things work out for us. God guides us through every problem with His word. He brings people and resources into our lives to help us with all of our needs and anything that concerns us. God does this because He created us to love and enjoy. We are God's hands in the world. He is looking for people that He can use to get things done in the Earth.

Being a vessel for God is the greatest joy in my life and it has allowed me to have a wonderful life even when things are going on in my life. His peace allows me to maintain a positive attitude and keep my joy. Once you have God's peace, you will have to fight to keep it because everything and everyone will try to take it from you. Peace will allow you to face what ever comes your way because you have God walking with you every step of the way.

THE SOLUTION TO ANY PROBLEM

Because of the awesome work that God has called us to do, we cannot do it apart from having a relationship with Him. The attack against women is too great. God is our lifeline. He is the only One who can guide us safely through every challenge we will face in life. God's love heals us and makes us whole. It is through His love that we are able do all the work He has called us to do. Our strength, power and wisdom come from God, as we pray and seek Him for help. God is the only consistent help that is available to us 24 hours a day. He allows us to come to Him just the way we are. He is the One who can tell us who He created us to be. God is the only One who has all knowledge about everything. He knows our yesterdays our today and our tomorrows. He is the only One who can give us the victory over all of our trials and tribulations. He has the power to work on our behalf and move the mountains we face. God loves you so much and there is nothing that you can do to stop Him from loving you!

We start our relationship with God when we receive Jesus as our Lord and Savior. Jesus gives us access to God the Father. All of us have sinned against God. This is noted in Romans 3:23 in the Holy Bible: "For all have sinned and come short of the glory of God." Sin is anything against God's word, which is disobedience. The consequence of sin is death. If we die in sin, we will be eternally separated from God. Sin must be paid for before we can have a relationship with God. We cannot be good enough to pay for the sin we commit against God. Sin can only be paid for with the blood of someone who has not sinned, and that person is Jesus Christ.

God gave his Son Jesus as a ransom to pay for the sins of everyone in the world because God loves us so much. The Bible teaches us in Romans 6:23: "For the wages of sin is death; but the gift of God is eternal life through Christ Jesus, our Lord." Jesus is the only way we can get to Heaven. When we accept what Jesus did for us on the Cross, which was paying the price we owed to God for sinning against Him, we are saved and we then become a part of God's family.

You can receive the free gift of Salvation today by admitting you are a sinner. Understand that as a sinner, you deserve death. Believe Jesus Christ died on the Cross to save you from sin and death. Repent by turning from your old life to a new life in Christ. Receive through faith in Jesus Christ His free gift of Salvation.

Pray this prayer and you will start your personal relationship with God: *Dear Lord, I admit that I am a sinner. I have done many things that don't please you. I have lived my life for myself. I am sorry and I repent. I ask you to forgive me. I believe that Jesus died on the Cross for me, to save me. You did what I could not do for myself. I come to you now. Take control of my life. I give my life to you. Help me to live every day in a way that pleases you. I Love You, Lord, and I thank you that I will spend all eternity with you. Amen.*

If you accepted the Lord Jesus today, welcome to the family of God. Reach out to someone and tell them about your decision. Then locate a church that teaches God's word so you can grow and enjoy the life that God has just given you. Allow God to heal you and help you live the life that He has planned for you. Read your bible daily. Meet together with other people who believe in Jesus. Get involved in a ministry group. Talk to God every day and enjoy your new life. You are a new creature in Christ. Old things have passed away and all things have become brand new. Get ready for a life that you never dreamed possible! God bless you!

Chapter Seven

Together We Stand

❄

MAP TO WHOLENESS

Wholeness is a journey and it is very personal. In my life, I've learned that there are levels of love for self just like there are levels of love for others. Many of us have a basic love for self. We love ourselves enough to wake up in the morning and brush our teeth, take a shower or bath, comb our hair, and iron our clothes before we leave the house. However, when we get to another level of love for ourselves, we learn to value ourselves enough to do those things that promote our well being. I've discovered that most of us are unable to care for ourselves on the same level that we care for others. Therefore, I believe it is necessary for each of us to help the other take better care of ourselves. We have to be tricked into caring for ourselves by telling ourselves that we are doing it for the people we care about. When we care for ourselves, we are healthy enough to continue caring for our love ones. I've also found that many of us do not get medical, dental, eye or GYN exams even though many of us have medical insurance. This is just the thing that a sister circle is best suited for.

Here is how we can use the sister circle to help each of us. If you do not already have a circle of women as your sister circle, look around at the women you do have in your life and select a few that would be open to getting together to start a sister circle with you. Let each of them know that you are forming the circle to give and receive help and support from each other for the purpose of obtaining a better quality of life. Now that you have your sister circle, call them all together to discuss some of the pressing issues that each of you are facing at this time in your lives. Remember everyone will have to warm up to sharing what's in their hearts. Therefore, let your need for better health and wellness guide the discussion. Now, exchange names and telephone numbers. After that, explain that each of you is required to make appointments to get an annual physical, dental, eye, GYN exams and a mammogram. When the appointments are made, each person is to call the other women in the circle to give them the dates of one another's appointments. Three days prior to each appointment, everyone is to call the person with the upcoming appointment to remind her about her appointment. This will ensure that each woman receives the necessary care she needs for her own well-being. To bond with each other, keep in touch by telephone on a weekly basis and get together a couple times a month to help each other stay on top of the challenges that each of you will face throughout the month. As your relationship grows, allow time for all of you to go on an outing together such as dinner, lunch or shopping. Then be prepared to live your life on a whole new level!

As women, there are many things that we would like to change in our lives. However, change is not easy. Many of us want to lose some weight so that we can look sexier in our clothes. However, we will only maintain the weight loss for a short while. In order to achieve and maintain weight loss and any other real improvement, we have to allow health and wellness to be the reason for what we do for ourselves or we will go back to the same bad habits.

Everything that we want to do first starts with a decision to do it. In order to do the things we want to, we must change our thinking about the thing first. When our thinking changes, the way we interact with ourselves also changes. We begin to make choices and decisions that show we care about ourselves as much as we care about others. We then need to get information on the topic of choice by reading books and talking to people who can offer successful ways to accomplish what we are trying to do. Success will come as long as you persevere and maintain your focus. Always remember why you are doing what you are doing. Keep the desired outcome in front of you at all times. Do not allow yourself to become side tracked with other things that compete with what you are trying to achieve. Change people, places and things that do not support the goal you are working towards. If you do not, you will be fighting an uphill battle with them and yourself. Take one step towards your goal each day and celebrate that step. Remember that every goal takes time to achieve so don't beat yourself up for any setbacks that you face.

You can ensure your success by giving yourself a longer time frame in which to accomplish your goal. Keep people around you that genuinely want you to reach your goal. Their support will allow you to start again after any disappointments. Love yourself at all times and remember to be your own best friend. Best friends do not call their friends names or make their friends feel bad about themselves. Create a schedule during the week that is blocked out just for you to work on your goal. Take pictures along the way so that you can see your progress. Reward yourself with something that will encourage you to continue the journey. Tell yourself on a daily basis that you are worth all of the work and you will be able to enjoy all of the benefits that comes with it. Pray for strength and a determined spirit to go all the way no matter what. You Go Girl, should be your cheer every step of the way. I know that you will reach every goal and dream that you have in your heart. I celebrate you where you are and where you will be! Now go for it!!!!

WE ARE ONE

Women are connected together because of our assignment. We are designed to be a unified force that is able to impact change for the betterment of all. None of us can exist without the other. As I noted earlier, we are our sister's keeper! If one of us is hurting, we all hurt. It is our strength to endure pain that brings us into unity. The journey of womanhood is different for each of us. However, the process involves going to God to understand why we went through all of the trials that we did. God is the only one who can give us the meaning for those experiences so that we can find our way to our ultimate destination, wholeness and purpose. When we take our brokenness and pain to God, He gives us His love and the strength to complete the healing process. We do this by helping others who are going through the same things that we have been through. Yes, we are to leave our problems and go and help someone else solve theirs. When we reach out to help others, God gives us victory in our lives. It allows us to take the focus off of our own problems. When we focus on ourselves, things are made worse because we think about our problems all day and all night. We then talk to others about it all the time and that only magnifies the problem which makes it seem 100 times worse than it actually is. Because of this, we are paralyzed and weighted down with a lot of stress. We are no longer able to do what we are charged to do, but thank God for the sisters in our lives. They are truly the wind beneath our wings that empower us to greatness and destiny. Never forget when you are feeling alone that you have a whole world full of women who are fighting the good fight with you, and for you. Remember, we are in this together and no one or nothing can defeat us when we stand together and support one another! I need you and you need me. Let us celebrate our uniqueness and come together to make the difference that only women can!

HELP FOR THE MISSION

Now that we understand that the process of woman-hood is best experienced with other women. Let us get to the bigger purpose for why we are women. As you can see, our world is getting more and more out of control. The structures that guided us for decades are almost non-existent. Many of our families are disconnected and hate is running rampant in our society. Parents are killing their children. Children are killing their parents. Husbands are killing their families. Many of the values that help shape our country are now replaced with vulgarity. Many of our teenagers are out of control and they are rebelling against every authority. It seems that no one is doing anything to make a real difference. There are many causes for the state of our world today. However, the largest reasons for the problems we are facing are directly related to women because we are out of position. Many of us decided to befriend our children instead of training them. We gave them lots of things without allowing them to earn them. We took on two and three jobs to keep our kids in the most fashionable clothes, the latest shoes, cell phones, and anything else they wanted. We were motivated to have our children become more rounded, so we put our children in too many activities. Now we live our lives catering to them by driving them to all of their activities. Therefore, we no longer have a life that allows us to rest and replenish ourselves from all of the long hours we work. We have worn ourselves out working all of those hours and our children raised themselves with the assistance of TV, music and their peers.

As women, we now know the solutions for the pain that we are having and how to start the healing process for every area of our lives. We are now in a position to be the women that God has created us to be, the most important person in our home. We have the power and the ability to turn our world around and save our children and our men. When we are in position, our women's intuition allows us to see things before they happen. We have a direct line to God at all times. Our prayers intercede on behalf of our families and our world. We are the ones who give strength, direction, guidance, support, and care to the world. Women are the greatest gift that God has given to humanity. We must never be complacent and unproductive. The world needs us to be whole, focused and determined to make this world a place where love and appreciation can override the hate and indifference that is currently trying to destroy it. Now that you have the right images of yourself just know that you are greater than what you used to be. You are better than what you use to have and you are worthy of the best that you can receive. Now go out and change the world! Our families are counting on us!

About the Author

❋

C heryle T. Ricks is a mother of four, the grandmother of six, a writer, a poet, motivational speaker, an Evangelist, a paralegal and a minister at Faith Church Baltimore in Baltimore Maryland.

She is a native Baltimorean who has lived in many different stations of life. She is an Alumna of Baltimore City Community College and Morgan State University.

Cheryle has allowed God to heal her soul. She has spent many years ministering to women at different stages of their lives with the sole purpose of helping them see their value and worth by teaching them how to receive real love, in spite of the abuse or the circumstances that they have been through. As a woman who has experienced abuse and no self esteem herself, she understands the importance of having the appropriate validation every woman needs. Her insight enables women to gets to the root cause for the emptiness that many women feel by helping them see the reality of their realities. Cheryle has learned through her relationship with God that there is nothing that can disqualify anyone

93

from having the life that Jesus Christ died for all of us to have. Motivated by the love of God, Cheryle shows women how to receive healing and restoration by taking the time to process those life challenges that they have left unresolved for most of their lives while walking with each of them every step of the way.

Let me first say that I have read this book as a man and I found it a joy and an honor to do so! It was the first book I ever read that presented a diagram for life, the process of life and real tools to handle the problem both as an individual and as a team. Thank you for writing this MASTERPIECE!

-Bishop Matthew E. Bradby, II

I have read many books over the years including many of the Classics that have been very helpful to me. I found this book to be enjoyable, enriching and encouraging. However, It is not just for women. It contained many life lessons for any human being going through the maze of life. It is a practical and spiritual guide to the well-being for both men and women. In my case, I married hastily in my youth and regretted my decision. If I had read this book before marrying, I could have avoided much heartache.

-Francis C. Snyder